Masters of Spinjitzu

WORLD OF NINJAGO
OFFICIAL GUIDE

BY TRACEY WEST

SCHOLASTIC INC.

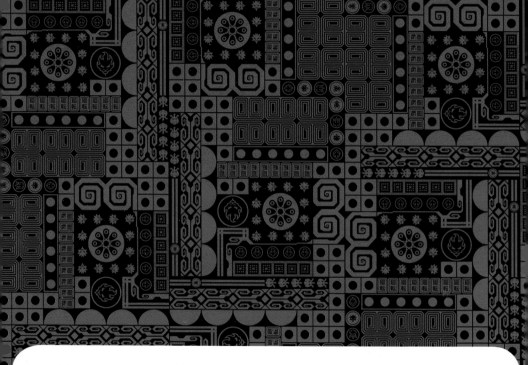

Published by Scholastic Inc., *Publishers since 1920*. SCHOLASTIC and associated logos are trademarks and/or registered trademarks of Scholastic Inc.

The publisher does not have any control over and does not assume any responsibility for author or third-party websites or their content.

This book is a work of fiction. Names, characters, places, and incidents are either the product of the author's imagination or are used fictitiously, and any resemblance to actual persons, living or dead, business establishments, events, or locales is entirely coincidental.

ISBN 978-0-545-80813-2

10 9 8 7 6 5 4 3 2 1   15 16 17 18 19/0

Printed in China   95
This edition first printing 2015

CONTENTS

WHAT'S NEW WITH THE NINJA?

When Zane sacrificed himself to save Ninjago™ from the Digital Overlord, it shook the ninja team to their cores. Cole, Jay, and Kai left to find other jobs. Only Lloyd remained determined to bring the team back together.

Then Master Chen invited all four ninja to the Tournament of Elements, and a clue led them to believe that Zane was alive somewhere on Chen's island. They entered the tournament, which pitted Elemental Masters against one another in battle. The ninja soon found Zane, but they lost their powers as they were swept up in Master Chen's sinister plan to raise an army of fierce Anacondrai warriors.

Defeating Master Chen was one of the ninja's greatest challenges — and a new challenge faced them, too. As Chen was swallowed into the Cursed Realm, a ghostly spirit named Morro, Master of Wind, escaped. Morro has a long history with Sensei Wu — and an evil plot of his own. The ninja would have to find new ways of fighting ghostly enemies.

In this guide, you'll find out how the ninja are changing to adapt to new challenges. You'll meet new villains and explore new places. There is a whole new world of Ninjago to explore!

The Ancient Art of Airjitzu

By now, everyone has heard of Spinjitzu, the ancient martial art that allows a ninja to become a tornado of elemental power. Cole, Jay, Kai, Lloyd, and Zane have mastered Spinjitzu, and now they have something new to learn: Airjitzu!

Imagine being able to jump up and fly over the head of your opponent during a martial-arts battle. You could avoid attacks, or launch a surprise attack from overhead. That is the power of Airjitzu. Those who master the art can take flight during a fight.

The mysterious Sensei Yang created Airjitzu years ago. He was a strict teacher, and legends say his teaching style drove away many pupils. Others say that his students were never seen leaving his temple. Was something sinister going on?

Sensei Yang passed on, leaving the secrets of Airjitzu behind on a scroll. These days, tour guides bring curious visitors to Yang's Haunted Temple.

In order to defeat Morro, the ghostly Master of Wind, the ninja had to seek out the scroll and learn Airjitzu. But their new skill alone would not be enough to stop Morro from unleashing terror on Ninjago . . .

My name is Sensei Wu.

I have been honored with the task of training and advising Cole, Jay, Kai, Zane, Lloyd, and now, Nya. They are all Elemental Masters, and I am proud they use their powers to protect Ninjago from evil forces.

The ninja are always discovering new things about their powers. I have created this history for them — and for you — so that they may know their past in order to prepare for the future.

IN THE BEGINNING . . .

There was my father, the First Spinjitzu Master. He created the four Golden Weapons of Ninjago and used them to build Ninjago. Then the evil Overlord attacked Ninjago with his Stone Army, and my father defeated them. He cast the evil half of Ninjago, the Dark Island, into the sea.

GARMADON'S STORY

My brother, Garmadon, and I had a happy childhood. Then Garmadon was bitten by a snake known as the Great Devourer. The snake's venom slowly turned him evil. He sought out a sinister teacher, Master Chen, who trained him until he became Lord Garmadon. At Chen's prodding, Garmadon intercepted a letter I sent to the woman we both loved, Misako. Garmadon signed the letter, and Misako married him instead of me.

MY STORY

With my love lost, I guarded the Golden Weapons and became a sensei. My first pupil was a young boy named Morro. I discovered he had an amazing power — he was a Master of Wind. I thought he might be the legendary Green Ninja, and I told him so. That was a terrible mistake. For when destiny did not choose Morro, he became consumed with a desire for power. He vanished while searching for the tomb of my father, the First Spinjitzu Master.

THE SERPENTINE WAR

For years, we believed the tribes of snakes known as the Serpentine waged war on Ninjago for their own gain. We have recently discovered that the Serpentine felt their safety was threatened, and wanted a truce with the people of Ninjago. Master Chen lied to them and told them a truce was not possible. He hoped to lead the Serpentine to victory and rule Ninjago.

Thanks to the Sacred Flutes, the Serpentine were defeated. The tribes were locked in tombs. Master Chen was exiled to an island. And the Seven Anacondrai Generals leading the Serpentine army were given the strictest sentence: They were banished to the Cursed Realm.

THE GOLDEN WEAPONS

As time passed, Lord Garmadon became completely controlled by evil. He tried to take the Golden Weapons for himself. I banished him to the Underworld and hid the weapons in four secret locations.

But my brother would not be stopped. He sprouted two new arms so that he could wield the four weapons at once. When I learned that he was putting together a skeleton army I knew I needed help. I sought out four young Elemental Masters — Cole, Jay, Kai, and Zane — to help me protect them.

MY PUPILS

I trained Cole, Jay, Kai, and Zane in the ancient art of Spinjitzu. I also taught them how to unleash their elemental powers. While I was instructing the ninja, Kai's sister, Nya, was training to become Samurai X.

When Lord Garmadon escaped from the Underworld, my pupils were ready to face him. Then a new student needed my help: my nephew, Lloyd

Garmadon. This young boy thought he was destined to follow in the evil footsteps of his father. But Lloyd is good at heart, and he soon realized the error of his ways — but not before he accidentally released the Serpentine from their underground prison.

THE GREAT DEVOURER AWAKENS

This was a time of many discoveries. Zane learned that he was a Nindroid, a robot created by the inventor Dr. Julien. We also learned that Lloyd was the true Green Ninja, destined to battle his own father. But Lloyd was not yet ready for that fight.

Pythor, the last surviving Anacondrai, awakened the Great Devourer — the same enormous snake who had bitten my brother. The only way to defeat the Great Devourer was with the Golden Weapons. We had to let Garmadon use his four arms to wield them. He was victorious, and the Great Devourer swallowed Pythor.

LLOYD CHANGES

Still evil, Lord Garmadon used the Golden Weapons to create a Mega Weapon that could create or destroy anything. He brought back to life an extinct ninja-hunting creature called the Grundle. To defeat the Grundle, Lloyd drank a tea that transformed him from a boy into a young man.

A NEW STAR

Lord Garmadon took the Mega Weapon back in time, and the ninja followed him. There they used the four Golden Weapons from the past to destroy the Mega Weapon. The Weapons became one and launched into space, forming a new star.

THE OVERLORD RETURNS

My brother's thirst for power remained unquenched. He raised the Dark Island and the Overlord, the evil force that had battled our father for control of Ninjago.

Lord Garmadon and the Overlord returned to Ninjago. The venom of the Great Devourer brought the Overlord's Stone Army back to life. It looked like Ninjago would be lost to darkness.

THE BIRTH OF THE GOLDEN NINJA

The ninja found the Temple of Light and unselfishly gave up their elemental powers so that Lloyd could become the Golden Ninja. In this new, ultimate form, Lloyd was powerful enough to battle his father.

Amazingly, Garmadon realized he did not want to fight Lloyd. But the Overlord possessed his body, transforming him into a huge black dragon. Lloyd was forced to battle his father. During the battle, he became the Ultimate Spinjitzu Master and created a Golden Dragon. He defeated the Overlord, and all the evil left his father.

NINJAGO REBOOTED

After the Overlord was defeated, everything changed. My brother became Sensei Garmadon, a peaceful teacher. Stripped of their elemental powers, Cole, Jay, Kai, and Zane became teachers at my school. Inventor Cyrus Borg infused Ninjago City with technology.

Then the spirit of the Overlord leaked into cyberspace, and the Digital Overlord was born. He forced Borg to create an army of evil Nindroids based on Zane's blueprints. The Digital Overlord had one goal: to use the power of the Golden Ninja to return to physical form!

POWERS LOST — AND RETURNED

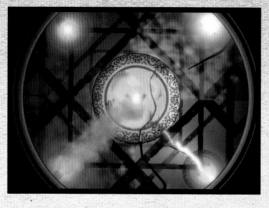

The Digital Overlord found a new supporter: Pythor, who had survived being swallowed by the Great Devourer. His scales were now white, but he was still intent on getting revenge on Ninjago. He and the Digital Overlord captured Lloyd and used his Golden Powers to bring the Overlord back into the real world.

To stop him, Lloyd did the only thing he could: He gave up his Golden Powers. Elemental powers returned to Cole, Jay, Kai, and Zane. They discovered they could use their powers even without the Golden Weapons.

ZANE'S SACRIFICE

The Overlord did not give up. He traveled to the star created by the original Golden Weapons and used them to create a suit of indestructible armor. The Golden Master could not be defeated — or could he?

That is when Zane performed an act of ultimate bravery. His friends captured, Zane latched on to the Golden Master. He called on his mysterious power source — the power of his heart. It grew and grew until it exploded, destroying the Golden Master. We all mourned Zane that day. It appeared as though he was lost forever. But that was not the case . . .

THE TITANIUM NINJA

Zane rebuilt himself into a stronger, smarter Nindroid: the Titanium Ninja. But my old enemy, Master Chen, captured him and his Nindroid friend, Pixal. In the years spent on his island, Master Chen had built a huge empire. It appeared to be a friendly noodle business, but in reality, Chen was creating an army of Anacondrai worshippers.

THE TOURNAMENT OF ELEMENTS

Master Chen planned to steal the powers of all the Elemental Masters so he could transform himself and his army into Anacondrai. With their new, powerful serpent bodies, they could take over Ninjago.

To get all the masters in one place, Chen organized the Tournament of Elements. The descendants of Elemental Masters came from all over Ninjago to see which one of them was the best.

The ninja had reason to believe that Zane was alive somewhere on Master Chen's island. They entered the tournament, accompanied by Sensei Garmadon.

THE NEW ANACONDRAI

The ninja tried to defeat Master Chen, but they failed. An Anacondrai army tore across Ninjago. To stop them, Sensei Garmadon opened the Cursed Realm and released the ghosts of the Seven Anacondrai Generals. My brother risked everything to save Ninjago, and he succeeded.

But something else escaped from the Cursed Realm — something dangerous. The ghost of my first pupil, Morro, emerged with a thirst for power and revenge. He conjured a crew of ghostly enforcers to help him.

A NEW NINJA IS BORN

How can the ninja battle that which has no form? Only one element can stop it: water. That is why Misako and I told Nya the truth about her family. Her mother was the Master of Water, and Nya has the potential to become the Ninja of Water.

Nya would rather remain Samurai X. Her need to succeed at everything she does hurts her training. But Nya must find her true potential, or Morro and his ghosts will plunge Ninjago into eternal darkness . . .

MEET THE NINJA

AND FRIENDS

In the beginning, the ninja team was Cole, Jay, Kai, and Zane, and their teacher, Sensei Wu. Since then, more friends have joined in the battle against evil. That's a good thing, because the bad guys keep getting badder — but the ninja and their friends keep getting stronger!

"Wu once said that the best way to defeat your enemy is to make him your friend . . . but how are you supposed to defeat your friend?"

ole versus Jay in battle? In an attempt to divide the ninja, Master Chen forced them to go head-to-head in the Tournament of Elements. At first, the battle was heated — until Cole and Jay realized that they could defeat Chen by sticking together and ending the match in a tie. But when Chen wanted them *both* eliminated, Cole took the fall for his friend.

"Cole may be gone, but he did not lose," declared Sensei Garmadon. "Let what he did here today be a lesson for us all: Know thy enemy, but more important, know thy friend. He fought like a ninja."

That's the kind of ninja Cole is. He thinks of his teammates before he thinks of himself. Cole is strong and dependable, and is always reliable in a fight.

Cole has never been truly appreciated as a leader — but that changed after he was eliminated from the Tournament of Elements. Stripped of his powers and forced to work in Chen's underground noodle factory, Cole began to search for his lost friend, Zane. Then he led the other elemental fighters in a daring escape plot.

ELEMENT: Master of Earth

BATTLE MOVES: Causes earthquakes, tosses heavy boulders as casually as baseballs

STRENGTHS: Superstrong, focused, and levelheaded

WEAKNESS: A fondness for cake

ole proved he had all the right moves when he helped
e ninja win a dance contest by performing the Triple
ger Sashay.

When the ninja team disbanded, Cole put his
muscles to work as a lumberjack.

Cole let Jay win their battle in the Tournament
of Elements . . .

. . . but he made up for it when he found Zane in
the tunnels under Master Chen's palace.

"I love roller skates. Did I ever mention I once placed first in the Mother-Son Skate-Off? . . . I should never have admitted that."

If there were such a thing as an Element of Talking, Jay would be master of it. In stressful situations, he'll always break the tension with a joke. But Jay's fast-talking sometimes gets him into trouble.

"I tried to warn you, but you never listen," Cole told Jay. "Talk? Yes. Listen? Not so much."

Jay is also lightning fast when it comes to problem solving. He's a talented gadget inventor, and he's always coming up with ideas to get the ninja out of tough spots.

In the Tournament of Elements, Jay had it easy when his first opponent left the competition early. Jay was ready to sit back and relax — until Master Chen put him against Cole.

At first, Jay was up for the fight. Jay used to date Nya . . . until a computer told Nya that Cole was her perfect match. Nya grew confused about her feelings, and Jay blamed Cole for betraying him. The Tournament of Elements was just the arena to settle the score.

But Jay and Cole soon realized the real enemy was Master Chen — not each other. Cole lost the fight on purpose so that Jay could continue. And Jay went on to fight harder than ever to make sure his friend's sacrifice was worth it.

JAY

ELEMENT: Master of Lightning

BATTLE MOVES: Lightning punch, throwing nunchuks

STRENGTHS: Superspeed, quick-thinking, fast-talking

WEAKNESS: Freaks out easily

Jay's Greatest Moments

One of Jay's first inventions was a pair of mechanical wings. When he first met Sensei Wu, he was testing them — but he ended up crashing into a billboard.

A bite from a Fangpyre once started to turn Jay into a snake, but a kiss from Nya cured him.

Before Lloyd got the ninja back together, Jay took a job as host of the game show *Ninjaaa . . . Now!*

Clouse's dark magic made him a fierce opponent, but Jay bravely took him on in a battle in the jungle on Master Chen's island.

"I will never turn on my friends."

KAI

The Tournament of Elements got complicated for Kai when he fell for Skylor, the Master of Amber. She is Master Chen's daughter, and she got caught up in her father's plans to steal the fighters' elemental powers.

When Master Chen saw Skylor had feelings for Kai, he decided to bring Kai over to his side. He offered to share dark secrets about Kai's parents if Kai would join him.

Master Chen should have known better. Kai might be impulsive, and sometimes he acts without his teammates, but he would never betray his friends. In his heart, he knows that being part of a team is better than being alone.

That said, being part of a team is not always easy for Kai. Once, he was sure he was destined to become the Green Ninja, but he put aside his ego to let Lloyd take the lead.

ELEMENT: Master of Fire

BATTLE MOVES: Raising flames, wielding swords

STRENGTHS: Brave, never hesitates in the face of danger

WEAKNESS: Sometimes acts without thinking things through

Kai's Greatest Moments

Kai realized his true potential when he saved Lloyd from a volcano.

After Kai easily defeated Dareth, the ninja got to use Dareth's dojo.

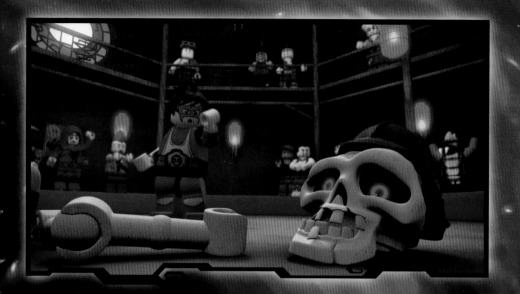

When the ninja disbanded, Kai found work fighting old enemies in an underground fight club.

Captured by Pythor, Kai bravely fought a one-man battle against the Nindroids.

When we thought we lost Zane, it nearly tore us apart, but we didn't quit. We let it fuel us.

loyd was very young when he became the Green Ninja, but he has always taken the responsibility seriously. He has never stopped training. When the evil left his father and Lord Garmadon became Sensei Garmadon, Lloyd began training with his dad.

After Zane sacrificed himself to save Ninjago from the Digital Overlord, the ninja left the team — everyone except for Lloyd. He wouldn't quit until he'd found all the ninja and brought them back together.

It was Lloyd's encouragement that kept the team together when it looked like they could never defeat Master Chen. Now that Morro has escaped from the Cursed Realm, Lloyd needs his teammates more than ever. Morro has possessed Lloyd's body. Lloyd is doing his best to fight it, but without the help of his friends, he might never break free from Morro's sinister hold.

LLOYD

ELEMENT: Master of Power

BATTLE MOVES: Powerful energy blasts; he can sometimes manifest his own Elemental Dragon.

STRENGTHS: Determination. Also, Lloyd does not abuse his great powers.

WEAKNESS: If Lloyd can't control his fear, his powers won't work.

Lloyd's Greatest Moments

After he left Darkley's Boarding School for Bad Boys, young Lloyd Garmadon went on a reign of terror in Jamanakai Village — demanding all the villagers' candy!

Nobody was more surprised than Lloyd when he learned he was destined to become the legendary Green Ninja.

During a battle with a crew of reanimated pirates, Lloyd unlocked his Spinjitzu for the first time.

To battle a ninja-hunting beast called the Grundle, Lloyd drank a tea that caused him to age instantly.

"I don't mean to boast, but I'm pretty good at most everything I pick up. Can you even count the times I've had to rescue the boys?"

Nya is a ninja of many faces. At first, the ninja knew her as Kai's little sister, kidnapped by the sinister skeleton Samukai. But Nya was much more than a helpless victim. She soon showed up as the mysterious Samurai X to help the ninja out of countless dangerous situations.

After they learned her secret, Nya became an important member of the ninja team. She keeps cool in dangerous situations, she can pilot any vehicle, and she's skilled at fixing things. There isn't much that Nya can't do. When the ninja entered the Tournament of Elements, Nya went undercover as a spy to help them.

After Morro escaped from the Cursed Realm, Sensei Wu and Misako told Nya some surprising news: Her mother was a Master of Water, which means that Nya is, too. And because water is the only element that can destroy ghosts, Sensei Wu began training her immediately.

But the training frustrated Nya. She's used to being good at things naturally. As she trains to become a Water Ninja, Nya will learn an important lesson about failure and success: Sometimes, failing is the only way to succeed.

ELEMENT: Samurai X / Master of Water

BATTLE MOVES: Launches nets and projectiles from her Samurai Mech. Her water moves are yet to be seen.

STRENGTHS: Nya is resilient, resourceful, and smart, especially when it comes to technology.

WEAKNESS: If Nya doesn't succeed right away, she gives up.

NYA

The ninja met Samurai X for the first time when Pythor pitted them against one another in the Slither Pit. After the battle, Kai saw Samurai X without a mask — and discovered that the fierce warrior was his sister, Nya!

Nya, evil? It happened once, when the Overlord's Dark Matter corrupted her.

Nya was dating Jay — until Cyrus Borg's "Perfect Match" machine told her that Cole was more compatible. Since then, she's been torn between two ninja!

To help save Zane, Nya went undercover in Master Chen's palace and discovered Clouse's spellbook.

"I am . . . the Titanium Ninja!"

When Zane first became a ninja, he had no memories of his past. His search for the truth led him to Dr. Julien, the inventor who'd created him. Zane was more than a ninja — he was a Nindroid!

In the battle with the Digital Overlord, Zane sacrificed himself to save Ninjago. His friends thought he was lost forever, and erected a titanium statue in his honor.

What the ninja didn't know was that Zane was rebuilding himself into a stronger, better Nindroid. But before he could reunite with his friends, he was kidnapped by Master Chen. He woke up in prison, where Master Chen was keeping him and Pixal in order to lure the other ninja to the Tournament of Elements.

At first, Zane didn't remember who he was. Pixal's voice guided him as he struggled to find his memories. Then they flooded back, and when Cole found Zane, he teamed up with his friend to help the elemental fighters escape from Master Chen's underground factory.

Now Zane is back and better than ever. He still doesn't know all the things his new titanium body can do. But he knows one thing for sure — he was, and always will be, a ninja!

ELEMENT: Master of Ice

BATTLE MOVES: Zane can shoot exploding shurikens from his wrists. His head can spin around 360 degrees.

STRENGTHS: This Master of Ice always keeps his cool when things heat up. He's got more stamina than the other ninja.

WEAKNESS: Until Zane discovered his humor switch, he never got any of his friends' jokes!

Zane's Greatest Moments

Thanks to a prank by Lloyd,
Zane's ninja suit turned pink.

Zane always knew he was different from other
ninja — and he discovered the truth about
himself when a mechanical falcon led him to the
workshop where his father had created him.

To save his new Nindroid friend, Pixal,
Zane gave up half his own power source.

To stop the Digital Overlord, Zane sacrificed
himself and saved Ninjago.

"There are things in my past I'm not proud of, but I don't regret them."

The ninja now known as Sensei Garmadon has taken many forms. Growing up, Garmadon was a promising ninja student, training with his brother, Wu, under their father, the First Spinjitzu Master.

Then the Great Devourer bit young Garmadon and infected him with evil. As Lord Garmadon, he had four arms so he could wield the four Golden Weapons. When the Overlord possessed him, he transformed into a dragon.

But Garmadon's son, Lloyd, destroyed the Overlord. Garmadon survived — and all the evil in him disappeared. His four arms were gone, too. Garmadon returned to a normal life with Misako and Lloyd.

That's when Garmadon became Sensei Garmadon. He opened a monastery to teach young students the art of fighting without fighting.

When Garmadon learned of Master Chen's Tournament of Elements, he had to help the ninja. Garmadon had sought guidance from Master Chen when he was a teen, and he knows how ruthless Chen can be.

When Master Chen cast a spell to turn himself and his followers into Anacondrai, Garmadon transformed once more, into Garma-Condrai. But even when things looked impossible, Garmadon did not stop fighting until he made sure that Ninjago was safe. He opened the Cursed Realm to release the Seven Anacondrai Generals — and was sucked inside. Will he be trapped there forever?

STRENGTHS: Garmadon's love for his son, Lloyd, and his ability to fight without fighting.

WEAKNESS: When Garmadon was young, his competitive feelings toward his brother led him to make some bad choices.

SENSEI GARMADON

Garmadon's Greatest Moments

For years, Lord Garmadon was banished to the Underworld — until he used the Golden Weapons to escape.

Lord Garmadon transformed the ninja's ship, the *Destiny's Bounty*, into the *Black Bounty*.

Lord Garmadon had the whole Stone Army under his command when he wore the Helmet of Shadows. (Later, bumbling ninja Dareth took control!)

Freed from the evil that gripped him for so long, Lord Garmadon became Sensei Garmadon and retreated to a monastery.

"With age comes wisdom."

Sensei Wu has been giving the ninja wise advice ever since he first brought them together. As a teacher, Wu passes on what he learned as a young boy from his father, the First Spinjitzu Master.

When the ninja went to Master Chen's island for the Tournament of Elements, Wu trusted that they were in good hands with his brother, Sensei Garmadon. He made plans to open his tea shop, Steap Wisdom, hoping to retire in peace.

But when Morro escaped from the Cursed Realm, Sensei Wu got swept into another battle to save Ninjago. Morro is seeking the tomb of the First Spinjitzu Master, which is said to hold massive power. Sensei Wu knows that the ninja can't defeat Morro without his help.

When he is not battling ghosts, Sensei Wu is doing what he does best — teaching. It's up to him to help Nya become a Master of Water, for only the power of water can defeat the ghosts. But Nya might just be his most difficult pupil yet. Can this expert teacher train the impossible student?

STRENGTHS: A combination of wisdom, experience, and kindness make Wu a great sensei.

WEAKNESS: Wu may be great at training ninja, but he doesn't know how to run a business.

Sensei Wu's Greatest Moments

Sensei Wu is a pretty serious teacher — but sometimes, even he likes to have fun.

Sensei Wu was almost lost forever when the Great Devourer swallowed him and Pythor while the two

Captured by the Nindroids, Sensei Wu became
the evil Tech-Wu, powered by the Digital Overlord's
sinister technology.

Wu revealed to Nya that he could manifest his own

"I need my puffy pot stickers!"

Never fear, the Brown Ninja is here!
Okay, maybe you should fear a little, because Dareth often makes a mess when he's trying to help. He's the founder of the Grand Sensei Mojo Dojo Academy, but when the ninja first met Dareth, they quickly discovered that he had no mojo at all.

While Dareth doesn't have mad skills like the other ninja, he has a big heart and is always ready to fight for what's right. Most of the time, he gets involved by accident.

Take the Tournament of Elements, for example. The reason Dareth came to Master Chen's island wasn't to rescue Zane, but to stop his favorite puffy pot stickers from being discontinued. He ended up finding Nya and almost blowing her cover. But he stuck around to help her and the ninja save the day.

STRENGTHS: Great hair and the ability to speak to sharks

WEAKNESS: Dareth thinks he's a much better ninja than he actually is.

"Aren't you going to kiss your mother good-bye?"

She might look like an ordinary working mom, but Misako has been entwined with the fate of Ninjago for a long time. In her youth, she was friends with Wu and Garmadon. Both brothers fell in love with her, but she married Garmadon — after he sent her a letter that Wu had written and claimed it as his own.

Misako went on to become an archaeologist for the Ninjago Museum of History. When her son, Lloyd, was just a baby, she learned that he would one day become the Green Ninja. Fearing for his safety, she left him behind to research how to prevent it.

But Lloyd's destiny could not be changed, and Misako returned to help her son in any way she could. Her knowledge helped the ninja defeat the Stone Army.

After the Digital Overlord was defeated, Misako helped Sensei Wu open his tea shop. And when Nya learns that she is a Water Ninja, Misako helps guide her. It is the best way she knows to save Lloyd, who is possessed by Morro's ghostly spirit.

STRENGTHS: Archaeology expert, levelheaded, gives good advice

WEAKNESS: She can be overprotective of Lloyd.

PIXAL

"Don't worry about me, Zane. I will always be a part of you."

Pixal first met the ninja when they came to visit her boss, Cyrus Borg, at his headquarters. Borg created the android to be his "Primary Interactive X-ternal Assistant Life-form." But the Digital Overlord infected her with evil and turned her against the ninja.

Zane immediately felt a connection with Pixal — he had never met another Nindroid like him before. He used his Techno-Blade to wipe out the evil program in her, and when she lost her power, he gave her half of his unique power source.

After Zane sacrificed himself to destroy the Digital Overlord, he woke up in a prison cell on Master Chen's island. He was confused, and his memory was faulty. Pixal's voice from the next cell helped him remember who he was.

When Zane escaped, he looked for Pixal — and found her scrapped on her cell floor. But he didn't leave her. He took the chip containing her neural drive and input it into his processor. Now Pixal is a voice in Zane's head, helping him calculate strategies and predict dangers.

STRENGTHS: Extensive data banks, loyal friend, great problem solver

WEAKNESS: Currently, she has no body of her own.

"I'm trying to make an honest living."

Ronin is a thief. Is he a good guy, a friend to the ninja, or a bad guy? Well, that's complicated — just like Ronin.

The ninja's search for the Ancient Scroll of Airjitzu led them to Ronin's shop in the village of Stiix. He greeted them by trying to capture them in a fishing net, which, of course, didn't work. Then he asked them to pay for the stolen scroll — and the ninja decided to steal it from him instead. But Morro beat them to it.

Ronin made a deal — he would tell the ninja another way to learn Airjitzu if they turned over their shares in Sensei Wu's tea shop to him.

Now Ronin is part of the ninja team, for better or worse. They're stuck with him — but can they trust him?

STRENGTHS: Charming, can talk his way out of tough situations

WEAKNESS: Untrustworthy

MEET MASTER CHEN

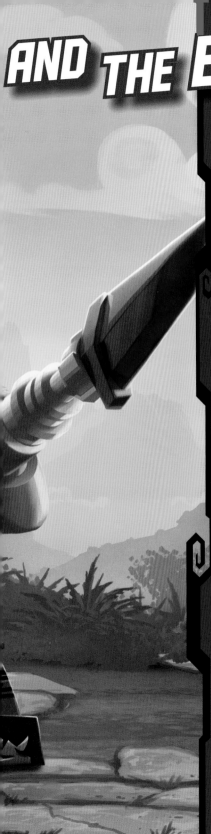

AND THE ELEMENTAL WARRIORS

When the ninja arrived on Master Chen's island, they were surprised they weren't the only ones in Ninjago with elemental powers. Everyone in the Tournament of Elements is a descendant of an original Elemental Master. These warriors were the guardians of the First Spinjitzu Master.

Each master's power had been passed down through the generations, and each one proved to be a skilled competitor. In the tournament, they would be forced to battle one another, one-on-one, until only one fighter remained.

What they didn't know was that Master Chen's tournament was just a trap — and a sinister fate awaited them all . . .

"When my followers become Anacondrai, Ninjago will be controlled by those who deserve it — the most powerful!"

Everyone in Ninjago knows Master Chen as the happy face behind Master Chen's Noodle House. But if they knew what truly lay behind his smile, they might lose their appetites.

For starters, Chen's noodles are made by captured slaves in an underground factory. And during the Serpentine Wars, Chen sided with the snakes. Chen was banished to his island, but he used it as an opportunity to create an evil empire. He dreams of a day when the Anacondrai will once again rule Ninjago.

"Master Chen is a dangerous man who should never be trusted. Whatever he promised you, do not believe him," Sensei Garmadon warned. But how does Garmadon know him so well? When Garmadon was training to be evil, Master Chen was his sensei!

And Garmadon was right. Chen's tournament was just a ploy to get all the Elemental Masters in one place. He wanted to steal their powers and use them to transform himself and his warriors into an army of Anacondrai.

"We will become the most powerful force Ninjago has ever seen!" Master Chen boasted. But he didn't count on one thing: He thought his tournament would divide the ninja — but it brought them closer together. When the ninja are a team, nothing can stop them!

ELEMENT: Master Chen is not an Elemental Master. That's why he needs to steal elemental powers from everyone else.

STRENGTHS: Chen is a master of trickery, of commanding his underlings . . . and of making tasty noodles.

WEAKNESS: Underestimating his opponents

SKYLOR

Skylor's power of absorption is impressive — once she touches another Elemental Master, she can copy their powers.

Kai was drawn to Skylor as soon as he met her. He thought she was a friend — until he discovered she was Master Chen's daughter. Skylor spied on the tournament competitors and told her father about the secret ninja alliance.

But Skylor isn't evil. Convinced that she couldn't do anything to stop her father, she went along with his plan. Then, when she realized that Kai and the ninja were trying to save Ninjago, she joined their side.

Like the other Anacondrai worshippers, Skylor has a snake tattoo on her back. After the spell was cast, Skylor transformed into Skylor-Condrai.

ELEMENT: Master of Amber

STRENGTHS: Skylor is a skilled fighter who easily adapts to the new powers she absorbs.

WEAKNESS: Believing she can't stand up to her father

CLOUSE

Creepy Clouse is a master of dark magic. He is fiercely loyal to Master Chen, even though Chen gave Garmadon the title of "Lord" instead of Clouse.

That left Clouse with a serious grudge against Sensei Garmadon — and he is one formidable enemy. Clouse can create spells designed to stop the ninja at every turn. He hurled balls of dark magic and created a large skull made of smoke that tried to swallow Nya whole. For a pet, he kept a giant purple snake with an appetite for ninja.

But Clouse's real target was Sensei Garmadon. His desire for revenge was greater than his loyalty to Master Chen. Locked in battle with Garmadon, Clouse opened up the Cursed Realm. He planned the ultimate punishment for Garmadon — but he didn't count on his old rival turning the tables on him.

> "I beg you, Master, let me use my sorcery and put an end to this."

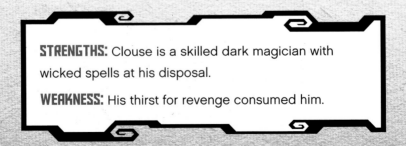

STRENGTHS: Clouse is a skilled dark magician with wicked spells at his disposal.

WEAKNESS: His thirst for revenge consumed him.

ZUGU

SERPENTINE FORM: ZUGU-CONDRAI

Twice the size of an ordinary man, former sumo wrestler Zugu is Chen's main muscle. He'll eat a plate of eggrolls for a light snack. He guards the workers in the noodle factory and bangs the gong every time Master Chen appears. He is one of Master Chen's generals.

"Now no one in Ninjago can stop us. *Ha-ha-ha-ha-ha!*"

EYEZOR

SERPENTINE FORM: EYEZOR-CONDRAI

Master Chen's other general, Eyezor, has only one eye, but makes up for it with toughness and brute strength. He sports a Mohawk, which makes him look extra bad. This might be one reason why Eyezor quickly rose in the ranks of Chen's minions.

"*Grunt!*"

KAPAU AND CHOPE

SERPENTINE FORMS: KAPAU-CONDRAI AND CHOPE-CONDRAI

These two Anacondrai worshippers gave themselves cool new names so Master Chen would notice them. Some might think that's a lousy strategy, but it worked. The bumbling minions were given more responsibilities, and when they transformed into Anacondrai, they gained awesome powers. But they quickly learned that when you make your way high in the ranks, it's a long way to fall when your leader fails.

"Look out, world. Kapau and Chope movin' up the ranks!"

PYTHOR

The only true surviving Anacondrai is Pythor P. Chumsworth, and he has shed his skin many times. After being sealed away in tombs with the other Serpentine, he was freed by Lloyd Garmadon. Pythor got the Serpentine together to raise the Great Devourer — but that backfired, and the mighty beast swallowed him.

Pythor survived, although his scales turned white. He tried to side with the evil Digital Overlord, but ended up becoming Mini-Pythor thanks to a shrinking pill meant for the Overlord. When the ninja found him again, he was living in a dollhouse inside Ninjago's prison.

Master Chen needed Mini-Pythor's essence to keep his army in snake form, but Mini-Pythor didn't want to help Chen. He thought Chen and his worshippers were impostors. And he was right. Chen might have sprouted scales and fangs, but he lacked one thing that Mini-Pythor has always had — a sense of honor.

"I really hate being small!"

ANACONDRAI WORSHIPPERS

Master Chen recruited an army of people willing to be transformed into Anacondrai to bring a new age to Ninjago. Turning into a snake might not sound like a great deal, until you consider the powers the Anacondrai have.

Each Anacondrai worshipper was marked with an Anacondrai tattoo on his or her back. When Clouse's spell was read, they began their transformation into scaly warriors. Then Master Chen sent his army out to terrorize Ninjago!

THE SEVEN ANACONDRAI GENERALS

With Pythor's help, Sensei Garmadon realized the only way to stop the army of Anacondrai was with true Anacondrai. Risking everything, Garmadon opened the Cursed Realm to release the spirits of the seven great Anacondrai generals. The serpents shot through every Anacondrai on the battlefield, turning them into ghosts. Chen and his false Anacondrai worshippers were banished to the Cursed Realm, and the spirits of the generals were finally free.

ASH, MASTER OF SMOKE

The Master of Smoke might not seem like a tough opponent — until you realize how hard it is to get your hands on him. Ash can turn into smoke, vanish, and reappear behind you in an instant.

"I'm up in smoke and gone with the wind."

BOLOBO, MASTER OF NATURE

This large, bearded warrior gets his powers from the earth. He channels them with his driftwood bo staff. When he plants his staff, roots and vines can spring up anywhere. Bolobo can control them and make them wrap around his opponents.

"This room could use a breath of fresh air!"

GRAVIS, MASTER OF GRAVITY

What goes up must come down — unless you're the Master of Gravity. Gravis can race up walls and across the ceiling. In battle, he floats and swoops through the air, levitating objects to launch his attacks.

"When I'm done with you, you won't know what's up or down."

GRIFFIN TURNER, MASTER OF SPEED

When it comes to fast-talking, Jay might have met his match in Turner. The Master of Speed likes to trash-talk his opponents as he zips and zooms around them. He's a high-energy fighter who went far in the tournament — and chose the right side when the time came.

"You can't lay a hand on me. I'm faster than fast. Swifter than swift."

JACOB, MASTER OF SOUND

Jacob may be blind, but that doesn't stop him from being a formidable fighter. He plays the sitar, and the sound he creates with it can shatter matter. He can take down opponents with his Sonic Scream. But while sound is his best weapon, it can also be his weakness. The noise of the rain distracted him during one battle in the tournament, and he lost.

JACOB HAS PERFECT AIM WITH A THROWING STAR.

"The minute you tell me the coast is clear, I'm bustin' outta here."

CHAMILLE, MASTER OF FORM

With her powers, Chamille can look like anyone she wants to. This helps her fool her opponents and catch them by surprise. Master Chen pitted Chamille against Lloyd in a Thunderblade battle. The other Elemental Warriors entered the roller-skating rink with them and could help — or hurt — whichever fighter they chose.

At first, the fighters sided with outgoing, confident Chamille, but in the end they chose to help Lloyd so he could continue on and take down Master Chen.

CHAMILLE CAN LOOK LIKE OTHER FIGHTERS, BUT SHE CAN'T COPY THEIR POWERS. ONLY SKYLOR CAN DO THAT.

"Watch your back, Green Ninja!"

KARLOF, MASTER OF METAL

When Karlof slams his metal fists together, he can turn his whole body into metal! Try making a dent in that. But Karlof is more than a hunk of steel. Back in his home of Metalonia, he used to be an aeronautical engineer. Down in the noodle factory, Zane asked Karlof to build a jet out of noodle-machine parts so the fighters could escape.

"Don't think Karlof afraid of you."

MR. PALE, MASTER OF LIGHT

An invisible ninja? That's Mr. Pale. When he's not battling, he walks around in a suit, glasses, and hat — but his body can't be seen. During a fight, he can make his clothes invisible, too. He sided with the ninja early on, but even his ability to become invisible didn't stop him from being imprisoned by Master Chen.

"You guys talking secret plans? I'm in!"

NEURO, MASTER OF MIND

Neuro has the ability to read minds. That's how he knows that the ninja aren't lying about Master Chen stealing everyone's powers. His special skills help the ninja stay one step ahead of Chen, but Jay is not super-impressed by his ability — he calls him "Nerdo."

Reading minds can be very useful in battle, however. Neuro can look into an opponent's thoughts and see an attack before it happens.

"Why would I help? You're the competition. The sooner you're out, the better for me."

SHADE, MASTER OF SHADOW

Shade's power allows him to disappear inside shadows. He can also move from shadow to shadow. This allows him to startle his opponents using the element of surprise.

You might think a shadowy guy wouldn't have a strong spirit, but Shade was determined to win the Tournament of Elements. He's a lone wolf who doesn't trust anyone.

"I ain't your spy, and I ain't your friend, either! That staff will be mine!"

TOX, MASTER OF POISON

Tox can release a green cloud of poison that makes her opponents sick. With her poisonous powers, she bravely fought with the ninja against the Anacondrai army.

"Do you feel me? Do you?"

Dragon Power

As the Green Ninja, only Lloyd had the power to manifest his Green Power Dragon just by thinking about it.

But when Zane became the Titanium Ninja, he began to be plagued by dreams of his Ice Dragon. The dreams terrified him. And then . . .

"I faced my fear," Zane said. "When I realized it wasn't something in front of me that held me back, but something inside me, I found a deeper power — a Dragon Power."

Zane flew in his Ice Dragon to help the ninja face Chen and his Anacondrai army. The other Elemental Fighters quickly realized that Zane had discovered the secret to unlocking their Dragon Powers: conquering fear.

One by one, the ninja and the Elemental Masters unleashed their Dragon Powers. Soon the skies were filled with a small army of Elemental Dragons racing across the sky.

MEET MORRO AND

THE GHOST NINJA

In order to vanquish Chen's Anacondrai army, Sensei Garmadon had to open the Cursed Realm. And Morro, the Master of Wind, escaped.

Morro had become a ghost, and he had a sinister plan. First, he would find the lost tomb of the First Spinjitzu Master. Then he would harness its power on Ninjago.

How can the ninja fight a ghost? Sensei Wu knows: "Water is the only weapon against a ghost. For though they can pass through solid objects, they cannot pass through what never stands still."

"Your powers are useless. You think you can hurt a ghost? I can possess

Like all ghosts, Morro was alive once. Sensei Wu took him in when he was a hungry street kid, and he became Wu's student. Morro did everything that was asked of him. Sensei Wu was impressed — especially when he saw that Morro had the power of wind.

"I thought I found the one," Wu said, thinking he had discovered the future Green Ninja.

When Wu told Morro of his possible destiny, Morro trained with an intense hunger. He became arrogant. Wu feared he had made a terrible mistake, but he knew it wasn't for him to decide — it was destiny.

And destiny chose. When Morro touched the four Golden Weapons, they didn't glow. Furious, Morro became determined to prove Sensei Wu wrong. He told Sensei Wu he'd find the tomb of the First Spinjitzu Master. Wu never saw him again.

Morro ended up in the Cursed Realm. When he escaped, he knew just who he wanted to possess: Lloyd, the Green Ninja. With his new, powerful body, he called up a ghostly team to help him with his goal: finding the lost tomb of the First Spinjitzu Master, and using its power to take his revenge on all of Ninjago!

MORRO

ELEMENT: Master of Wind

BATTLE MOVES: Morro can possess the body of any opponent he touches.

STRENGTHS: When he combines his ghostly powers with the stolen powers of the Green Ninja, Morro is practically invincible.

WEAKNESS: Morro should have thought twice before possessing Lloyd. While he gained power, Lloyd constantly fought the takeover, making Morro weak.

The Ghost Ninja

BANSHA

This white-haired ghost wields wicked blades, but her greatest weapon is her voice. With a sinister song, she can cause the earth to shake and snow to tumble down a mountain in a dangerous avalanche.

"I wiped them off the face of the mountain!"

GHOULTAR

This brutish ghoul might not be big on brains, but you wouldn't want to run into Ghoultar on a dark and stormy night — or any night, for that matter. He carries an oversized scythe, and he gets a big thrill out of possessing anyone and anything he touches.

"Me likes! Me likes to take! Take now!"

SOUL ARCHER

Soul Archer's weapon of choice is a ghostly bow and arrows. His arrow has a mind of its own, and can weave around obstacles to hit its target.

"Run, run, run away . . . My arrow will find you anyway!"

WRAYTHE

Sporting biker gear and riding a tricked-out ghoulish motorcycle, Wraythe is as bad as they come. He fights with a ghostly chain. If it touches you, he can send his energy through it and transform you into a ghost. Once, Wraythe got hit by a train — and was left without a scratch! (He is a ghost, after all.)

"Your world will pay when Morro finds the tomb!"

GEAR UP!

Knowing the Ancient Art of Spinjitzu and the newer art of Airjitzu are amazing skills for a ninja. But when you're battling opponents like Anacondrai warriors and ghosts, you need all the help you can get. A flying ship and armor that protects you from ghosts can come in handy.

You also need to know what gear your opponents are packing, so that you can come up with a strategy to fight them!

DEEPSTONE AEROBLADE

Regular weapons, no matter how powerful, can't damage ghosts. But Aeroblades can. They're made of Deepstone, an aquatic material mined from the bottom of the ocean. When an Aeroblade makes contact with a ghost, the ghost explodes into ethereal vapor. Then the Aeroblade returns to its owner, like a boomerang. The ninja first tried out their Aeroblades in a battle against ghost ninja conjured by Morro.

"It's official — Aeroblades are cool."
— Jay

THE NEW *DESTINY'S BOUNTY*

The ninja have a long history with this old ship. When they needed a home, Zane found the abandoned ship in a desert, and the ninja settled in. Then Jay modified the *Destiny's Bounty* and turned it into a flying machine. While they fought Lord Garmadon, the ship got hijacked, trashed, and crashed more times than the ninja could count.

　　When the *Destiny's Bounty* was left behind on the Island of Darkness, it looked like it was beyond repair. But unbeknownst to the ninja, Nya brought the old ship to her Samurai X lair and got to work repairing it. It took a long time, but the new *Destiny's Bounty* is better than ever, with a sleeker body and jet engines that can quickly propel it out of tight spots.

NYA'S MOBILE BASE

When Nya headed out to spy on Master Chen's evil empire, her mobile base was the perfect cover. She built it to replace the *Destiny's Bounty* until she could get the ship fixed, so she calls it "the DB Express."

A digital shield around the vehicle can make it look like a noodle truck, a school bus, a big rock — or whatever's needed to help the mobile base blend into its surroundings. In its basic form, it looks like an ordinary truck, but it's equipped with some amazing features: a tower turret, laser cannons, and a mini-robot copilot. Huge tires with big treads allow her to travel across all kinds of terrain.

The mobile base also has a great sound system, which is a bonus — unless you're trying to hide from Master Chen's minions and reveal your location by loudly blasting music (like Dareth did on Master Chen's island)!

RONIN'S AIRSHIP, *R.E.X.*

Ronin is not a ninja, but he uses his airship to help the ninja when they clash with Morro and his ghostly crew. It can speed through the air like a small jet and hover like a helicopter. If Ronin is in trouble, he can whistle, and the ship will come right to him.

SKYLOR'S HOVERBOARD

A flying skateboard? Escaping one of Clouse's dark magic attacks, Skylor activated a small device that transformed into a winged hoverboard! Skylor jumped on and flew away, spewing fire out of the hoverboard's jets.

ANACONDRAI SWORD

This sword was part of Master Chen's collection of treasures. The Anacondrai swords boasted the sharpest blades in existence. Chen's sword was plundered from the Anacondrai tomb after it was rediscovered. "Fit for the greatest warrior ever to do battle in Ninjago," Chen boasted.

BLADE CHARIOTS

These single-passenger vehicles look like wicked scorpions on wheels. Spinning blades whirl by the front left and right wheels. Master Chen's Anacondrai worshippers rode them.

JADE BLADE

In the Tournament of Elements, capturing a shimmering green Jade Blade was what would usually determine the winner of the battle. The first to grab the blade was spared the trapdoor.

"Behold — a Jade Blade. Here it represents life."
        — Master Chen

FANG BLADE

Another Anacondrai weapon, a Fang Blade is as sharp as a serpent's tooth. The Fang Blades are the original teeth of the Great Devourer, an enormous serpent who tried to consume all of Ninjago. The Anacondrai use them as weapons.

MASTER CHEN'S ZEPPELIN

When Master Chen needed to survey his island, he could take to the sky in this enormous balloon. He used it to get a bird's-eye view of the jungle when he had the Elemental Warriors track down Nya. It's also equipped with one of Chen's favorite features — trapdoors.

"That guy's love of trapdoors is seriously getting on my nerves!"
— Lloyd

STAFF OF ELEMENTS

The large crystal that tops this staff pulses hypnotically with a special power. With the help of Clouse's dark magic, Master Chen used the staff to drain the Elemental Warriors of their powers. Then he used the staff to create those powers in battle. Kai briefly wielded the Staff of Elements — and a darkness came over him that he couldn't control.

"The Staff of Elements holds the power of your fallen foes, and soon it'll hold all but one!"
— Master Chen

LOCATIONS

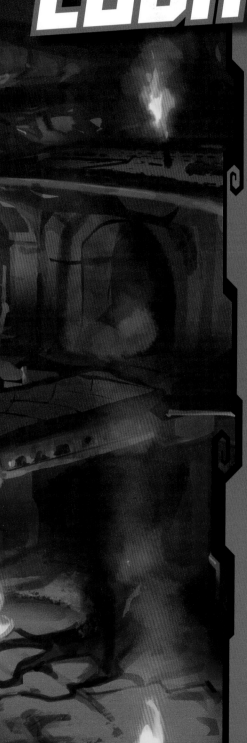

Ninjago is a vast and sprawling world. Each time the ninja begin an adventure, we learn about new and fascinating corners of this ancient land.

MASTER CHEN'S ISLAND

Banished to the island for siding with the snakes during the Serpentine Wars, Chen quickly began creating an empire all his own. The island is so secret that it doesn't show up on any known map.

"How is it we're on an island I've never seen on any map?"

— Kai

MASTER CHEN'S PALACE

The palace where the Tournament of Elements is held is a huge, impressive place. At first, Chen gave each fighter a room suited to their element and personality. In Jay's room, every device was configured to interact with his electrical signal. Cole's room had a whole cupboard full of Chinese food and cake.

But life in the palace was only good when Master Chen was happy. When he learned that the ninja and some of the warriors were conspiring against him, he transferred them to cold, bare barracks with uncomfortable beds.

THE TOURNAMENT ARENA

Master Chen really knew how to put on a show. In his Tournament Arena, the environment changed to fit the elements of the warriors battling each other. Fighters faced off in a temple dojo, a giant cherry blossom tree, a Zen rock garden, and a suspension bridge hanging over the mouth of a fiery volcano. When Chen pitted Lloyd against Chamille, Master of Form, in a Roller Derby–type race, the arena became the Thunderblade Arena.

THE PALACE TUNNELS

Losers in the tournament feel the floor disappear beneath them as they are sucked through a trapdoor into Master Chen's tunnels. It's a vast network of creepy spaces. There's the Anacondrai Temple, where the Anacondrai worshippers gather to watch Chen drain the fighters of their powers. Then the fighters are dragged away to Chen's underground noodle factory, where a team of captured workers toils day and night to make noodles for his popular restaurant chain.

The tunnels also hold prison cells for those Master Chen wants to keep a close watch on — like Zane.

And the creepiest thing in the tunnels isn't a place — it's an enormous purple snake. (Not as big as the Great Devourer, but still pretty big.) This purple beast is Clouse's pet, and he uses it to make sure nobody escapes this dismal dungeon.

THE JUNGLE

If you're lucky enough to escape Chen's tunnels, you'd still have to make your way through the thick jungle to find your way to shore. Master Chen has rigged the whole island with booby traps. Even if you manage to avoid them, you'd have to hack your way through giant plants and overgrown vines.

SAMURAI X CAVE

Samurai X is Nya's secret identity, so of course she needs a secret cave she can retreat to. There, Nya works on creating new vehicles, weapons, and gadgets for herself and the ninja. When the *Destiny's Bounty* crashed and was left to turn to dust, Nya rescued it, brought it back to her cave, and transformed it into a sleeker, better ship.

The cave is one reason that Nya loves being Samurai X. There's a part of her that worries that when she finally becomes the Water Ninja, she'll have to give up being Samurai X for good.

STEAP WISDOM TEA SHOP

Sensei Wu ran a monastery and a school for kids, and then he decided to start a tea shop. After all, he loves a good cup of tea. With Misako's help, he opened the shop, but he had a hard time attracting customers. When customers did show up, Morro and his ghostly crew scared them off.

Then Ronin became a partner in the business, and Sensei Wu didn't know what hit him. Ronin had a flashy business style and wanted to give the shop a new name, like "Shake-Your-Boo-TEA."

Running a tea business seemed more stressful than being a sensei. And at heart, Sensei Wu is, and always will be, a teacher.

THE CURSED REALM

This is one spot in Ninjago you definitely don't want to visit. It's where souls are punished for their bad deeds. After the Serpentine Wars, the Seven Anacondrai Generals were banished there. The members of the Elemental Alliance didn't realize the Anacondrai had asked for a truce — Master Chen tricked them.

That's why Garmadon released the generals from the Cursed
Realm to fight Chen-Acondrai and his army of transformed Anacondrai
worshippers. He saved Ninjago from Chen, but he paid a high price.
And unbeknownst to Garmadon, someone else escaped with the
generals — Morro, the Master of Wind. Now the ninja will have to figure
out how to reopen this impenetrable prison and send Morro back.

KRYPTORIUM PRISON

This isn't just any prison — it's home to Ninjago's worst of the worst. Some of the villains held there have included:

- Frakjaw, a warrior in the Skulkin army
- Captain Soto and his crew of reanimated pirates
- The Stone Warriors from the Overlord's army
- Pythor, the last of the Anacondrai

When Master Chen and his army broke into the prison to get their hands on Pythor, many of the inmates escaped and are on the loose. If they're captured again, Kryptorium Prison will be waiting for them.

CORRIDOR OF ELDERS

Walk down this narrow canyon passage, and you'll see that the legends of Ninjago are carved into the towering rock walls. Master Chen longs to see his face there.

THE LIBRARY OF DOMU

Inside this library, holy men in robes look after sacred scrolls encased in glass. The scroll containing the secrets to the Ancient Art of Airjitzu was kept there — until Ronin the thief stole it, hoping to sell it for a profit.

THE VILLAGE OF STIIX

This rickety village is suspended on towering stilts over the ocean, just off the coastline. If you don't watch your step on the creaky wooden walkways connecting everything, you'll fall three stories into the water below!

Stiix is no seaside resort. It's seen better days. Weatherworn windmills slowly turn in the breeze. Fishing nets hang from every dock. Scruffy-looking people sell trinkets and peddle gifts to the few visitors who travel there.

It's the perfect place for an unsavory thief like Ronin, who set up a shop in Stiix. And even though water is dangerous to ghosts, Morro and his crew decided to hide out there, too — after all, a village on the water is the last place the ninja would expect to see a ghost!

"Welcome to Stiix. Watch your step."
— a villager

THE GHOST NINJA

After the ninja defeated Master Chen and his army of Anacondrai worshippers, peace came to Ninjago. But it didn't last long. When Lloyd was lured to the Ninjago Museum of History, he faced a ghostly enemy with powers he had never seen before . . .

Being the night watchman at the Ninjago Museum of History was a boring job. During the day, crowds of people came to see the exhibits. They marveled at a model of the Great Devourer. They *oohed* and *ahhed* at Cyrus Borg's inventions.

But at night, everything was quiet. The night watchman had nothing to do but pace down the hallways. But sometimes, he liked to have a little fun.

The Seasons of the Ninja was his favorite exhibit. One display held models of all five ninja in action poses. Lloyd Garmadon, the legendary Green Ninja, was in the center.

Another display held models of villains. There was Lord Garmadon, with his four arms. And Master Chen, the evil noodle baron.

The night watchman borrowed a rubber sword from the souvenir stand. He poked at the Garmadon statue. "Ninjago won't be seeing the likes of you anymore! Good riddance!" he cried.

Whoosh! Something brushed behind the guard. He spun around.

"Who's there? The museum's closed," he called out.

There was no reply. But one by one, the exhibit lights went out. The night watchman fumbled with his flashlight.

"I know Spinjitzu!" he warned. His flashlight flickered.

Whoosh! Something brushed past him again. But what? He spun around, and his flashlight shone on . . . the model of Samurai X. The night watchman sighed in relief.

But something was still out there.

"I'm legally required to tell you that I've unlocked my true potential," the night watchman boasted.

This time, he heard a low, quiet laugh. An evil laugh. The night watchman grabbed his walkie-talkie.

"That's it, I'm calling this in —" he began, but then he stopped. A light shone on the ninja exhibit. The model of the Green Ninja had been torn apart. One arm was missing, and black spray paint had been scrawled across the uniform.

Whoosh! The night watchman spun around again.

This time, he saw something charging at him faster than the wind. He let out a scream.

"Aaaaaaaaaaaaaaaaaaaaaah!"

The next morning, the five ninja flew across the ocean on their Power Dragons. Lloyd and his Green Dragon took the lead. The Green Dragon swooped down and grazed his wing against the water, playfully splashing Kai.

Jay laughed. "That's one way to cool off a hothead!"

"No one messes up my hair!" Kai protested, but he was grinning. He steered his Red Dragon toward the water and tried to splash Lloyd. But Lloyd swiftly moved aside, and the water hit Zane instead.

"You okay there, Zane?" Cole called out.

"Affirmative," Zane replied. "It'll take more than a little water to take me out."

"What about a big fish?" Jay asked. "Incoming!"

An enormous fish with sharp fangs leaped out of the water. It tried to swallow Zane and his Ice Dragon in one gulp. But Zane and his dragon rolled away, and the fish splashed back down into the ocean.

Inside Zane's brain, he could see Pixal on his visual display.

"Based on its weight and size, this is the mutant Fangfish terrorizing the coastal village and depleting their food source," she reported.

"Pixal says this is the one," Zane told the others.

"Well, now that he's taken the bait, let's reel him in and get him to the aquarium," Lloyd suggested.

The ninja changed course, sweeping back toward the land. Beneath them, the Fangfish followed.

"Let me guess, Kai. You caught one that big once," guessed Jay.

"Heck no. He was *twice* that size!" Kai bragged.

The Fangfish leaped out of the water again, and Kai dodged it.

"He's almost as hungry as you, Cole!" Jay joked.

"And twice as ugly as you, Jay!" Cole shot back.

Lloyd got them back on track. "It's time for the catch of the day! In line formation!"

The ninja lined up, Lloyd at the front and Cole

bringing up the rear. The Fangfish chased after them. Just as it was about to leap out of the water again, the ninja flew to the left and right.

Whomp! The fish landed on the big, flat deck of a fishing boat. The crew of the boat cheered.

The ninja landed their dragons on shore. They helped the fishing crew get the enormous Fangfish onto an aquarium truck.

Kai and Lloyd watched a dad buy a fishing pole for his son.

"Looks like we've made this place fish friendly again," Kai said with satisfaction. "If your father were still here, he'd tell you he's proud. You've become a great leader, Lloyd."

Lloyd shook his head. "No, we're a great team," he insisted. He looked at the father and son and sighed. "Can't say I don't miss him. With my dad gone, sometimes I question where I'm going. Sometimes I worry about who I might become."

Kai nodded. "I know how that feels. After I lost my dad, I lost my way. But I was lucky to have a sister watch over me." He ruffled Lloyd's hair. "Don't worry, big shot. I'll watch over you from now on."

Lloyd playfully punched him. "No one messes up my hair."

With the job done, the ninja climbed on their dragons and took flight once more. They flew across the water to the rolling green farmlands of Ninjago. They set down in front of Sensei Garmadon's sanctuary — at least, that's what it used to be. Sensei Wu had transformed the place into a tea shop.

Sensei Wu painted the last brush stroke on the sign in front of the sanctuary. "Steap Wisdom," he said with a chuckle. "Not a bad name for a tea shop."

Inside the shop, Nya stocked the shelves with bottled tea as Misako organized the register.

"Steap Wisdom is starting to look like a real tea house, except for one thing — customers," Nya remarked.

"Good things come to those who wait," advised Sensei Wu.

The Ghost Ninja

Then they heard the ninja arrive outside. They were talking and laughing.

"Oh, who am I kidding?" Sensei Wu asked. "I'm tired of waiting. I'll put the ninja to work."

Cole, Jay, Kai, Zane, and Lloyd stepped inside.

"Ninja, you need to find customers," Sensei Wu said.

"No 'Hello, how's it going, glad to hear you saved the day again'?" Jay asked.

Sensei Wu ignored the ninja's protests. He gave each one a work uniform with the Steap Wisdom tea shop logo on it. Then he pointed to a tall stack of fliers.

"I want you to pass these out in the city," he instructed.

"No offense, Sensei, but aren't we going to look kinda dorky flying on our Power Dragons with these things on?" Kai asked.

"You won't be flying on anything," Sensei Wu replied. "We're selling tea, not magic. Besides, you all have been relying a little too heavily on your elemental powers lately. Real power comes from inside."

Lloyd grabbed some fliers. "It would be our honor, Sensei."

Just then the phone rang, and Misako answered. She listened, and then hung up the phone.

"It's the police," she said. "They've asked for Lloyd. There's been a break-in at the museum."

Kai took the fliers from him. "Go on. I'll take your share."

"I owe you one," Lloyd said, heading for the door.

"Aren't you going to kiss your mother good-bye?" Misako asked.

"Mom, we've talked about this," said Lloyd, embarrassed. "I'll catch you on the way back."

Lloyd made his way to Ninjago City. A break-in at the museum sounded like no big deal. He'd check it out, see how he could help, and then rejoin the ninja.

When he arrived, he ducked under police tape to enter the museum lobby. Two police officers were having a coffee break.

"Well, lookee here. The Green Ninja," said Officer Noonan. "Feel safer already."

"I got your call," Lloyd said. "Was there a break-in?"

"That night watchman over there had quite a scare,"

replied Officer O'Doyle. "Doesn't remember a thing."

He pointed toward a guy sitting with a blanket wrapped around him.

"Hasn't been too helpful. Maybe you'll have better luck," Officer Noonan said.

"Thanks," Lloyd said.

As he walked toward the night watchman, the two officers looked at each other.

"Did you make the call for him?" asked Officer O'Doyle.

"I didn't. Did you?" asked Officer Noonan.

"No," Officer O'Doyle replied. "Wonder who did?"

Lloyd slowly approached the night watchman.

"So you were on guard when it happened?" he asked.

The night watchman didn't reply. He just sipped his coffee.

"Can you show me what was stolen?" Lloyd asked. "I'm here to help you."

The guard looked at Lloyd curiously. Then he nodded. "Follow me."

He stood up and shuffled off down the hallway. Lloyd followed him down a staircase into what looked like a storage room. The place was filled with crates. Some were opened, and Lloyd could see ancient-looking objects inside them.

"I was knocked out," the night watchman

explained. "When I came to, I found the only thing stolen was something that wasn't even on display."

He pointed to an opened crate. Sand spilled out, but that was all that was inside.

"Just a worthless old armored breastplate they call the Allied Armor of A'Zure," the night watchman said.

Lloyd looked around the room. Some of the objects looked like they were made of silver and gold.

"Why would a thief leave these priceless relics and take just that?" Lloyd wondered. He knelt down to examine the open crate.

"Oh, I don't know," the night watchman said from behind him. "Maybe it's because when you're in trouble, they say it's got the power to summon allies, whether they be friends, foes, or even spirits from the Cursed Realm."

"The Cursed Realm? My father is there," Lloyd said. He turned to look at the watchman.

The night watchman had an axe raised above his head! And his blanket had fallen off, revealing that he wore an armored breastplate.

Lloyd reacted with lightning speed as the axe came down. He quickly rolled to the right, dodging the attack.

"The Allied Armor . . . you stole it?" he asked.

The watchman turned, bringing down the axe once more. This time, Lloyd jumped up on top of a crate and then flipped off of it.

"So Wu chose you to be the beloved Green Ninja?" the guard asked. "Silly old man."

He swung the axe again, and Lloyd dodged it.

"How do you know Sensei?" Lloyd asked. "And if you've got a bone to pick with me, perhaps we can discuss things *without* the sharp weapons? I don't want to hurt you."

The watchman lunged again, and Lloyd knew he had no choice. He whirled into a Spinjitzu tornado, knocking the guard out cold. Lloyd looked at his still body, relieved.

Suddenly, white, misty vapors flowed from the watchman's body. They flowed into a portrait of Master Chen. The painting came to life!

"Spinjitzu isn't going to be enough to stop me!" the painting cried.

Lloyd stared at the painting, confused. Then he noticed that the night watchman was sitting up.

"What's going on?" the guard asked. "Someone was in my head."

Then Lloyd got it. That misty vapor — whatever it was — was his real opponent. Not the night watchman.

Zap! He hurled a bolt of energy at the painting. It evaporated instantly. But the vapor survived. It snaked across the room to a bronze statue of a Serpentine. The snake statue came to life.

"Your powers are useless," it told Lloyd. "You think you can hurt a ghost? I can possess anything!"

A ghost! Lloyd realized. None of his training had prepared him for this. Still, he had to try to fight it.

The Ghost Ninja

But the statue wrapped its cold, bronze tail around Lloyd, gripping him tightly. Then the vapor flowed out of the statue into the sand that had spilled onto the floor. Before Lloyd's eyes, the sand took the shape of a ninja.

Keep it together, Lloyd, he told himself. *This ghost likes to talk. Maybe he'll say something that can help you defeat him!*

"You're a ghost from the Cursed Realm," Lloyd said as the creepy sand ninja stepped toward him. "How did you escape?"

"When your father opened a door, he should have been more careful about what came out," said the sand ninja. Then he lunged.

Zap! Lloyd sent a burst of energy toward a nearby vacuum. It sucked up the sand.

Lloyd quickly slithered free from the serpent statue's grasp. Then he ran to the night watchman.

"Hurry, the Allied Armor — give it to me!" Lloyd urged.

The watchman fumbled with the straps. His hands were shaking.

"When he was in my head, I saw his thoughts," the watchman said. "The world . . . the world will be cursed!"

He handed over the armor just as the vacuum bag exploded.

"Behind you!" the guard yelled.

Lloyd spun around. Violent winds swirled around him, and a ghostly ninja formed out of the vapors. A scar ran across his face.

"You can't have the armor!" Lloyd yelled over the wind.

"The armor's nice, but it's not the only thing I want to possess," the ghost ninja said.

"What else do you want?" Lloyd asked.

The ghost grinned. "You," he replied.

Whoosh! Lloyd felt the ghost ninja charge at him. He couldn't move. He couldn't fight.

Then everything went black.

THE WORLD WILL BE CURSED!

After Morro possessed Lloyd's body, the ninja lost their powers. Morro used the Allied Armor to conjure up a ghostly army. The ninja will have to defeat Morro to save their friend — and once again, save Ninjago.

First they must master the Ancient Art of Airjitzu. Nya must learn to become the Master of Water. But most important, they must work together. Every member of the team is important.

Can they do it? Will the ninja be able to save Lloyd? And if they do, how will they get Morro back to the Cursed Realm? It won't be easy, but if there's one thing we know for certain, it's that ninja never quit!

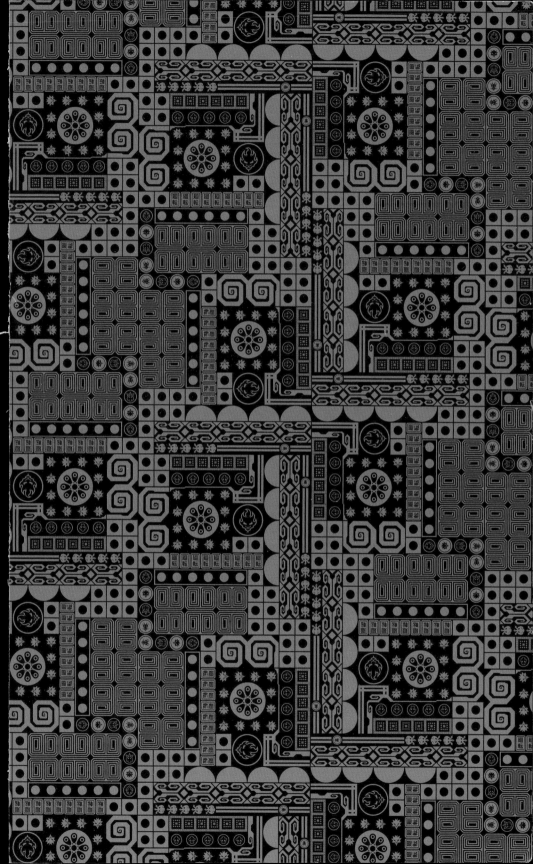

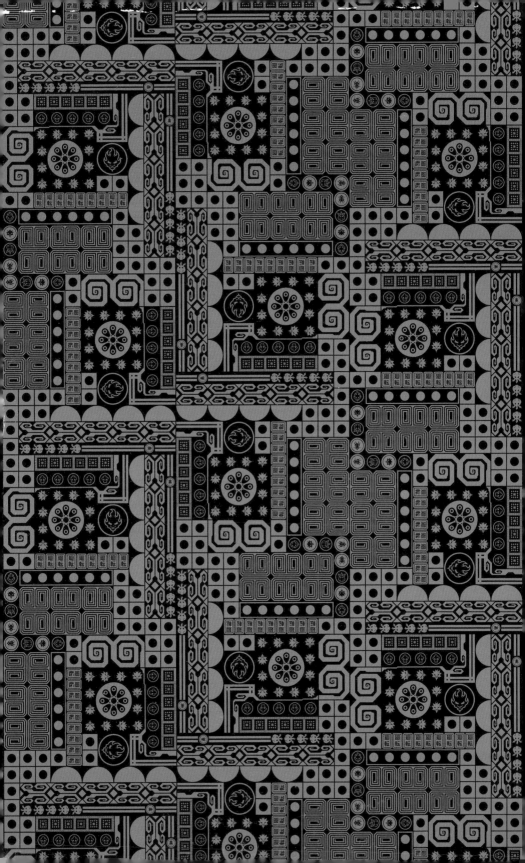